This journal belongs to

....

Date

....

*T*he Lord your God is with you.... He will quiet you with his love.

ZEPHANIAH 3:17 NIV

You are a beloved child of God,
precious to Him in every way. As you seek Him, He will show you
the mysteries of life and unfold His unique plans for you—
a life full of rich blessing.

God cares about you and knows all the desires of your heart.
He is as close as breathing. Let this journal inspire you to express
your thoughts, record your prayers, embrace your dreams,
and listen to what God is saying to you.

Be strong in the Lord, and may His presence guide your heart always.

Be Still and Know

Bestow upon me, O Lord my God, understanding
to know Thee, diligence to seek Thee, wisdom to find Thee,
and a faithfulness that may finally embrace Thee.

THOMAS AQUINAS

Perhaps this moment is unclear, but let it be—even if the next,
and many moments after that are unclear, let them be.
Trust that God will help you work them out, and that all the unclear
moments will bring you to that moment of clarity and action
when you are known by Him and know Him.
These are the better and brighter moments of His blessing.

WENDY MOORE

We must concentrate on knowing God; the more
we know Him the more we want to know Him. And as knowledge
is commonly the measure of love, the deeper
and wider our knowledge,the greater will be our love.

BROTHER LAWRENCE

They who seek the throne of grace
Find that throne in every place;
If we live a life of prayer,
God is present everywhere.

OLIVER HOLDEN

_Be_ still, and know that I am God!

PSALM 46:10 NLT

Audience of One

Solitude liberates us from entanglements by carving out a space
from which we can see ourselves and our situation before
the Audience of One. Solitude provides the private place where we can
take our bearings and so make God our North Star.

Os Guinness

Solitude begins with a time and place for God, and God alone.
If we really believe not only that God exists but also that He
is actively present in our lives—healing, teaching, guiding—we need to
set aside a time and space to give Him our undivided attention.

Henri J. M. Nouwen

When you pray, go away by yourself, shut the door behind you,
and pray to your Father in private. Then your Father,
who sees everything, will reward you.

Matthew 6:6 nlt

You have set Your glory above the heavens.
Thy glory flames from sun and star:
Center and soul of every sphere,
yet to each loving heart how near.

Oliver Wendell Holmes

*W*hen we focus on God, the scene changes. He's in control of our lives; nothing lies outside the realm of His redemptive grace.

PENELOPE J. STOKES

Sharing with God

Prayer is such an ordinary, everyday, mundane thing. Certainly, people who pray are no more saints than the rest of us. Rather, they are people who want to share a life with God, to love and be loved, to speak and to listen, to work and to be at rest in the presence of God.

ROBERTA BONDI

God still draws near to us in the ordinary, commonplace, everyday experiences and places.... He comes in surprising ways.

HENRY GARIEPY

There is an essential connection between experiencing God, loving God, and trusting God. You will trust God only as much as you love Him, and you will love Him to the extent you have touched Him, rather that He has touched you.

BRENNAN MANNING

The impetus of God's love comes from within Himself, to share with us His life and love. It is a beautiful, eternal gift, held out to us in the hands of love. All we have to do is say "Yes!"

JOHN POWELL

I'll lead you to buried treasures, secret caches of valuables—
Confirmations that it is, in fact, I, GOD...who calls you by your name.

ISAIAH 45:3 MSG

The Best Times

When you open up the Bible and you pray the Scriptures back to God,
you're experiencing something really wonderful.... He's delighted.
The silence confirms that we are His people. We are talking
and God is listening. But the best times are when God starts talking,
and we're quiet enough to hear Him.

CALVIN MILLER

That is God's call to us—simply to be people who are content
to live close to Him and to renew the kind of life in which
the closeness is felt and experienced.

THOMAS MERTON

I have set the LORD always before me....
Therefore my heart is glad and my tongue rejoices;
my body also will rest secure....
You have made known to me the path of life;
you will fill me with joy in your presence,
with eternal pleasures at your right hand.

PSALM 16:8–9, 11 NIV

The kiss of eternal life, and the warm embrace of God's Word,
are so sweet, and bring such pleasure, that you can never
become bored with them; you always want more.

HILDEGARD OF BINGEN

*I*t is God's love for us that He not only
gives us His Word but also lends us His ear.

DIETRICH BONHOEFFER

Blessed Assurance

So wait before the Lord. Wait in the stillness.
And in that stillness, assurance will come to you.
You will know that you are heard; you will know that
your Lord ponders the voice of your humble desires;
you will hear quiet words spoken to you yourself,
perhaps to your grateful surprise and refreshment.

AMY CARMICHAEL

In those times I can't seem to find God,
I rest in the assurance He knows how to find me.

NEVA COYLE

Peace *with* God brings the peace *of* God. It is a peace
that settles our nerves, fills our mind, floods our spirit,
and in the midst of the uproar around us, gives us
the assurance that everything is all right.

BOB MUMFORD

Do not be anxious about anything, but in everything,
by prayer and petition, with thanksgiving, present your requests to God.
And the peace of God, which transcends all understanding,
will guard your hearts and your minds in Christ Jesus.

PHILIPPIANS 4:6–7 NIV

$\mathcal{B}$e assured, if you walk with Him and look to Him
and expect help from Him, He will never fail you.

GEORGE MUELLER

Fill Me Up, Lord

When I am in solitude, the presence of God is so real and so full
that there is nothing else I want. The people I love are with me
in God's presence, beyond the surface choppiness of all the stresses
that separate us as finite beings on this earth, and I am able
to experience our ultimate togetherness in God. This experience
is absolutely the only thing that fills the longing of my heart.

RUTH HALEY BARTON

The LORD will guide you always;
he will satisfy your needs in a sun-scorched land
and will strengthen your frame.
You will be like a well-watered garden,
like a spring whose waters never fail.

ISAIAH 58:11 NIV

Prayer is to the spirit what breath is to the body.
We treat prayer as though it were the spice of life,
but the Bible prescribes it as a vital staple in our diet.

DAVID HUBBARD

Solitude is for those with an ample interior, with room to roam,
well-provided with supplies. And I need a day or two,
every so often, to make the journey.

CATHERINE CALVERT

Our love to God arises out of our emptiness;
God's love to us out of His fullness.

HANNAH MORE

Only in Silence

If we really want to pray, we must first learn to listen:
for in the silence of the heart, God speaks. And to be able to see
that silence, to be able to hear God, we need a clean heart.
Let us listen to God, to what He has to say. We cannot speak
unless we have listened, unless we have made our connection with God.

MOTHER TERESA

It is in silence that God is known,
and through mysteries that He declares Himself.

ROBERT H. BENSON

I wait quietly before God,
for my victory comes from him....
Let all that I am wait quietly before God,
for my hope is in him.

PSALM 62:1, 5 NLT

If Jesus Christ is bringing you into the understanding
that prayer is for the glorifying of His Father,
then He will give you the first sign of His intimacy—silence.

OSWALD CHAMBERS

There is a silence into which the world cannot intrude.
There is a peace you carry in your heart and cannot lose.

We receive only when we are recollected; only in silence
is heard the beating of the heart of God.

FATHER BERNARDO OLIVERA

The Desire to Know

In extravagance of soul we seek His face. In generosity of heart,
we glean His gentle touch. In excessiveness of spirit,
we love Him and His love comes back to us a hundredfold.

TRICIA MCCARY RHODES

Late have I loved You,
O beauty so ancient and so new.
Late have I loved You!
You were within me while I
have gone outside to seek You.
Unlovely myself, I rushed towards
all those lovely things You had made.
And always You were with me.

AUGUSTINE

If we really want to know God, we will seek Him. As we start
to enjoy His divine companionship, experience His peace,
and trust His direction, we will crave more of Him
in every area of our lives. We will come to a place where He will
ask us what we want, and we will simply say, "You, Lord—
not your blessings, not what you can do for us—only You."

AMY AND JUDGE REINHOLD

*K*eep on asking, and you will receive what you ask for. Keep on seeking, and you will find. Keep on knocking, and the door will be opened to you.

MATTHEW 7:7 NLT

A Centered Life

Life from the Center is a life of unhurried peace and power.
It is simple. It is serene.... We need not get frantic.
He is at the helm. And when our little day is done,
we lie down quietly in peace, for all is well.

THOMAS R. KELLY

Drop thy still dews of quietness
till all our strivings cease;
take from our souls the strain and stress,
and let our ordered lives confess
the beauty of Thy peace.

JOHN GREENLEAF WHITTIER

Because we are spiritual beings...it is for our good, individually
and collectively, to live our lives in interactive dependence upon God.

DALLAS WILLARD

There is nothing but God's grace. We walk upon it; we breathe it;
we live and die by it; it makes the nails and axles of the universe.

ROBERT LOUIS STEVENSON

For of Him and through Him and to Him are all things,
to whom be glory forever. Amen.

ROMANS 11:36 NKJV

*F*or in him we live and move and have our being.

ACTS 17:28 NIV

Rhythms and Patterns

In waiting we begin to get in touch with the rhythms of life—
stillness and action, listening and decision. They are the rhythms
of God. It is in the everyday and the commonplace
that we learn patience, acceptance, and contentment.

RICHARD J. FOSTER

Love comes while we rest against our Father's chest.
Joy comes when we catch the rhythms of His heart.
Peace comes when we live in harmony with those rhythms.

KEN GIRE

In the process of creation and relationship, what seems mundane
and trivial may show itself to be holy, precious, part of a pattern.

LUCI SHAW

It's in Christ that we find out who we are and what we are living for.
Long before we first heard of Christ and got our hopes up,
he had His eye on us, had designs on us for glorious living,
part of the overall purpose he is working out
in everything and everyone.

EPHESIANS 1:11–12 MSG

Get the pattern of your life from God,
then go about your work and be yourself.

PHILLIPS BROOKS

The patterns of our days are always changing...rearranging...
and each design for living is unique...graced with its own special beauty.

Prayer Is...

Prayer is the deliberate and persevering action of the soul. It is true and enduring, and full of grace. Prayer fastens the soul to God and makes it one with God's will, through the deep inward working of the Holy Spirit.

JULIAN OF NORWICH

We pray not to get something, but to open up a two-way street between us and God, so that we and others may inwardly become something.

JOHN HEUSS

Prayer is neither chiefly begging for things, nor is it merely self-communion; it is that loftiest experience within the reach of any soul, communion with God.

HARRY EMERSON FOSDICK

Our Father in heaven,
Hallowed be Your name.
Your kingdom come.
Your will be done
On earth as it is in heaven.
Give us this day our daily bread.
And forgive us our debts,
As we forgive our debtors.
And do not lead us into temptation,
But deliver us from the evil one.
For Yours is the kingdom
and the power and the glory forever.
Amen.

MATTHEW 6:9–13 NKJV

The possibilities of prayer run parallel with the promises of God.
Prayer opens an outlet for the promises...and secures their precious ends.

E. M. BOUNDS

Wait on the Lord

God never abandons anyone on whom He has set His love;
nor does Christ, the good shepherd, ever lose track of His sheep.
How slow we are to believe in God as God, sovereign, all-seeing
and almighty! We need to "wait upon the Lord" in meditations
on His majesty, till we find our strength renewed
through the writing of these things upon our hearts.

J. I. PACKER

Those who wait on the LORD
Shall renew their strength;
They shall mount up with wings like eagles,
They shall run and not be weary,
They shall walk and not faint.

ISAIAH 40:31 NKJV

When I need a dose of wonder I wait for a clear night
and go look for the stars.... In the country the great river
of the Milky Way streams across the sky, and I know that our planet
is a small part of that river of stars.... Often the wonder of the stars
is enough to return me to God's loving grace.

MADELEINE L'ENGLE

$\mathcal{Y}$ou are a little less than angels, crown of creation, image of God.
Each person is a revelation, a transfiguration,
a waiting for Him to manifest himself.

EDWARD FARRELL

Approach the Throne

I don't know, when I'm asking for something here on earth,
what is going on in the innermost shrine of Heaven (I like to think about
it, though). I am sure of one thing: it is good. Because Jesus
is there. Jesus loves me. Jesus has gone into that shrine on my behalf.
The hope we have is a living hope, an unassailable one.
We wait for it, in faith and patience.

ELISABETH ELLIOT

If you keep this comparison always in mind—that of a castle
with a wondrous throne within—God may use it to draw you
into His presence, where He bestows the favors that He loves to grant.

TERESA OF AVILA

I lift up my eyes to the hills—
where does my help come from?
My help comes from the LORD,
the Maker of heaven and earth.

PSALM 121:1–2 NIV

God is always on duty in the temple of your heart, His home....
It is the place where Someone takes your trouble
and changes it into His treasure.

BARBARA JOHNSON

I lift up mine eyes to the quiet hills, and my heart to the Father's throne;
in all my ways, to the end of days, the Lord will preserve His own.

TIMOTHY DUDLEY-SMITH

Our Gracious God

The grace of God means something like: Here is your life.
You might never have been, but you *are* because the party
wouldn't have been complete without you. Here is the world.
Beautiful and terrible things will happen. Don't be afraid.
I am with you. Nothing can ever separate us. It's for you
I created the universe. I love you.

FREDERICK BUECHNER

God makes everything come out right;
he puts victims back on their feet....
As high as heaven is over the earth,
so strong is his love to those who fear him.
And as far as sunrise is from sunset,
he has separated us from our sins.

PSALM 103:6, 11–12 MSG

His overflowing love delights to make us
partakers of the bounties He graciously imparts.

HANNAH MORE

The joyful birds prolong the strain,
their song with every spring renewed;
the air we breathe, and falling rain,
each softly whispers: God is good.

JOHN HAMPDEN GURNEY

Grace means that God already loves us
as much as an infinite God can possibly love.

PHILIP YANCEY

*L*ord...give me only Your love and Your grace.
With this I am rich enough, and I have no more to ask.

IGNATIUS OF LOYOLA

Delight in the Lord

Trust in the LORD and do good;
dwell in the land and enjoy safe pasture.
Delight yourself in the LORD
and he will give you the desires of your heart.
Commit your way to the LORD;
trust in him and he will do this:
He will make your righteousness shine like the dawn,
the justice of your cause like the noonday sun.
Be still before the LORD and wait patiently for him.

PSALM 37:3–7 NIV

God's pursuit of praise from us and our pursuit of pleasure in Him
are one and the same pursuit. God's quest to be glorified and our quest
to be satisfied reach their goal in this one experience:
our delight in God which overflows in praise.

JOHN PIPER

I rejoice in following your statutes
as one rejoices in great riches.
I meditate on your precepts
and consider your ways.
I delight in your decrees;
I will not neglect your word.

PSALM 119:14–16 NIV

_I_ delight to do Your will, O my God,
And Your law is within my heart.

PSALM 40:8 NKJV

Take Time

Intimacy may not be rushed.... We can't dash into God's presence
and choke down spiritual inwardness before we hurry
to our one o'clock appointment. Inwardness is time-consuming,
open only to minds willing to sample
spirituality in small bites, savoring each one.

CALVIN MILLER

It may seem strange to think that God wants to spend time with us, but...
think about it. If God went to all the trouble to come to earth,
to live the life that He did, to die for us, then there's got to be a hunger
and a passion behind that. We think of prayer as an "ought to,"
but in reality it is a response to God's passionate love for us.
We need to refocus on the fact that God is waiting for us to show up and
be with Him and that our presence truly touches Him.

DR. HENRY CLOUD

Come and sit and ask Him whatever is on your heart.
No question is too small, no riddle too simple.
He has all the time in the world.
Come and seek the will of God.

MAX LUCADO

I've loved you the way my Father has loved me.
Make yourselves at home in my love.

JOHN 15:9 MSG

He Comes in Stillness

He doesn't come in the roaring thunder, as we expect.
He doesn't write in blazing lightning as it flashes across the clouds,
even though we watch for Him there. His voice won't be in
the rushing wind or in the pounding rhythm of the waves breaking
against the seashore. He simply comes to us in a still small voice.

WENDY MOORE

We may ask, "Why does God bring thunderclouds and disasters
when we want green pastures and still waters?" Bit by bit,
we find behind the clouds, the Father's feet; behind the lightning,
an abiding day that has no night; behind the thunder, a still small voice
that comforts with a comfort that is unspeakable.

OSWALD CHAMBERS

"Go out, and stand on the mountain before the LORD."
And behold, the LORD passed by, and a great and strong wind
tore into the mountains..., but the LORD was not in the wind;
and after the wind an earthquake, but the LORD was not
in the earthquake; and after the earthquake a fire, but the LORD
was not in the fire; and after the fire a still small voice.

1 KINGS 19:11–12 NKJV

The lightning and thunder, they go and they come,
But the stars and the stillness are always at home.

GEORGE MACDONALD

God Is Great

The simple fact of being...in the presence of the Lord
and of showing Him all that I think, feel, sense, and experience,
without trying to hide anything, must please Him. Somehow,
somewhere, I know that He loves me, even though I do not feel
that love as I can feel a human embrace, even though I do not hear
a voice as I hear human words of consolation.... God is greater
than my senses, greater than my thoughts, greater than my heart.
I do believe that He touches me in places
that are unknown even to myself.

HENRI J. M. NOUWEN

Have you ever thought what a wonderful privilege it is that
every one each day and each hour of the day has the liberty of asking God
to meet him in the inner chamber and to hear what He has to say?

ANDREW MURRAY

The LORD your God is with you....
He will take great delight in you,
he will quiet you with his love,
he will rejoice over you with singing.

ZEPHANIAH 3:17 NIV

*G*od is the sunshine that warms us, the rain that melts the frost
and waters the young plants. The presence of God
is a climate of strong and bracing love, always there.

JOAN ARNOLD

He's Near

The God who made the world and everything in it, this Master of sky
and land, doesn't live in custom-made shrines or need the human race
to run errands for him, as if he couldn't take care of himself. He makes
the creatures; the creatures don't make him. Starting from scratch,
he made the entire human race and made the earth hospitable,
with plenty of time and space for living so we could seek after God,
and not just grope around in the dark but actually find him.
He doesn't play hide-and-seek with us. He's not remote; he's near.

ACTS 17:24–27 MSG

God is not an elusive dream or a phantom to chase,
but a divine person to know. He does not avoid us, but seeks us.
When we seek Him, the contact is instantaneous.

NEVA COYLE

God proves to be good to the man who passionately waits,
to the woman who diligently seeks.
It's a good thing to quietly hope,
quietly hope for help from God.

LAMENTATIONS 3:25–26 MSG

_To seek God means first of all
to let yourself be found by Him._

Glimpses of Majesty

Worship the LORD in the splendor of his holiness;
tremble before him, all the earth.
Say among the nations, "The LORD reigns."
The world is firmly established, it cannot be moved;
he will judge the peoples with equity.
Let the heavens rejoice, let the earth be glad;
let the sea resound, and all that is in it;
let the fields be jubilant, and everything in them.
Then all the trees of the forest will sing for joy

PSALM 96:9–12 NIV

Forbid that I should walk through
Thy beautiful world with unseeing eyes:
Forbid that the lure of the market-place
should ever entirely steal my heart away from
the love of the open acres and the green trees:
Forbid that under the low roof of workshop
or office or study I should ever forget
Thy great overarching sky.

JOHN BAILLIE

The God who holds the whole world in His hands
wraps Himself in the splendor of the sun's light
and walks among the clouds.

Savor little glimpses of God's goodness and His majesty,
thankful for the gift of them.

Desert Bloom

The desert and the parched land will be glad;
the wilderness will rejoice and blossom.
Like the crocus, it will burst into bloom;
it will rejoice greatly and shout for joy....
They will see the glory of the LORD,
the splendor of our God....
Then will the eyes of the blind be opened
and the ears of the deaf unstopped.
Then will the lame leap like a deer,
and the mute tongue shout for joy.
Water will gush forth in the wilderness
and streams in the desert.

ISAIAH 35:1–2, 5–6 NIV

Every journey has a wilderness passage. Sometimes quite a few.
But as the path leads on, we discover that without the desert,
we do not fully experience the oasis.

BARBARA FARMER

See, I am doing a new thing!
Now it springs up; do you not perceive it?
I am making a way in the desert
and streams in the wasteland.

ISAIAH 43:19 NIV

*W*ithin each of us, just waiting to blossom,
is the wonderful promise of all we can be.

Fully Satisfied

O God, you are my God;
I earnestly search for you.
My soul thirsts for you;
my whole body longs for you
in this parched and weary land
where there is no water.
I have seen you in your sanctuary
and gazed upon your power and glory.
Your unfailing love is better than life itself....
I will praise you as long as I live.

PSALM 63:1–4 NLT

The Lord's chief desire is to reveal Himself to you and, in order for Him to
do that, He gives you abundant grace. The Lord gives you the experience
of enjoying His presence. He touches you, and His touch is so delightful
that, more than ever, you are drawn inwardly to Him.

MADAME JEANNE GUYON

Blessed are those who hunger and thirst for righteousness,
for they will be filled.

MATTHEW 5:6 NIV

Genuine heart-hunger, accompanied by sincere seeking
after eternal values, does not go unrewarded.

JUSTINE KNIGHT

Only God can fully satisfy the hungry heart.

HUGH BLACK

Experience Christ

I pray that from his glorious, unlimited resources he will empower you
with inner strength through his Spirit. Then Christ will make his home
in your hearts as you trust in him. Your roots will grow down into
God's love and keep you strong. And may you have the power
to understand, as all God's people should, how wide, how long,
how high, and how deep his love is. May you experience
the love of Christ, though it is too great to understand fully.
Then you will be made complete with all the fullness of life
and power that comes from God.

EPHESIANS 3:16–19 NLT

Let us continue to love each other since love comes from God.
Everyone who loves is born of God
and experiences a relationship with God.

1 JOHN 4:7 MSG

Once the seeking heart finds God in personal experience
there will be no problem about loving Him. To know Him
is to love Him and to know Him better is to love Him more.

A. W. TOZER

_T_his is how we know what love is:
Jesus Christ laid down his life for us.

1 JOHN 3:16 NIV

He Restores My Soul

The LORD is my shepherd, I shall not be in want.
He makes me lie down in green pastures,
he leads me beside quiet waters,
he restores my soul.
He guides me in paths of righteousness
for his name's sake.
Even though I walk
through the valley of the shadow of death,
I will fear no evil,
for you are with me;
your rod and your staff,
they comfort me.
You prepare a table before me
in the presence of my enemies.
You anoint my head with oil;
my cup overflows.
Surely goodness and love will follow me
all the days of my life,
and I will dwell in the house of the LORD
forever.

PSALM 23:1–6 NIV

The purpose of grace is primarily to restore our relationship
with God.... This is what all the work of grace aims at—an ever deeper
knowledge of God, and an ever closer fellowship with Him.

J. I. PACKER

My people will dwell in a peaceful habitation,
In secure dwellings, and in quiet resting places.

ISAIAH 32:18 NKJV

*Y*ou have made us for Thyself, O Lord; and our hearts
are restless until they find rest in Thee.

AUGUSTINE

Moments to Reflect

Much of what is sacred is hidden in the ordinary,
everyday moments of our lives. To see something of the sacred
in those moments takes slowing down
so we can live our lives more reflectively.

KEN GIRE

Reflection...enables our minds to be stretched
in three different directions—the direction that leads
to a proper relationship with God, the relationship that leads
to a healthy relationship with others, and the relationship
that leads to a deeper understanding of oneself.

MARK CONNOLLY

What we lack is not so much leisure to do as time to reflect
and time to feel. What we seldom "take" is time to experience
the things that have happened, the things that are happening,
the things that are still ahead of us.

MARGARET MEAD & RHODA METRAUX

What we feel, think, and do this moment influences
both our present and the future in ways we may never know.
Begin. Start right where you are.

ALEXANDRA STODDARD

*R*eflect on what I am saying,
for the Lord will give you insight into all this.

2 TIMOTHY 2:7 NIV

God Wants You

Listening to God is a firsthand experience.... God invites *you*
to vacation in His splendor. He invites *you* to feel the touch of His hand.
He invites *you* to feast at His table. He wants to spend time with *you*.

MAX LUCADO

The Most High calls to us and waits for us to respond.
He desires to quench our deepest thirst, to satisfy our deepest hunger,
and to fill us with His power and presence as we dwell
in the secret place of the Most High.

CYNTHIA HEALD

He is a God who can be found. A God who can be known.
A God who wants to be close to us. That's why
He is called Immanuel, which means "God with us."
But He draws close to us as we draw close to Him.

STORMIE OMARTIAN

Come near to God and he will come near to you.

JAMES 4:8 NIV

God is always speaking to us. Listen to Him.
He wants from us deep love, compassion, and forgiveness.

MOTHER TERESA

Through His Creation

In such a beautiful wilderness of wildflowers we are amused with the very
variety and novelty of the scene so much that we in our pleasure lose
all sense of weariness or fatigue in the length of our wanderings
and get to the end before we are aware of our journey.

JOHN CLARE

God's love is like a river springing up in the Divine Substance
and flowing endlessly through His creation,
filling all things with life and goodness and strength.

THOMAS MERTON

I am convinced that God has built into all of us an appreciation
of beauty and has even allowed us to participate in the creation
of beautiful things and places. It may be one way God brings healing
to our brokenness, and a way that we can contribute toward
bringing wholeness to our fallen world.

MARY JANE WORDEN

Our Creator would never have made such lovely days,
and have given us the deep hearts to enjoy them,
above and beyond all thought,
unless we were meant to be immortal.

NATHANIEL HAWTHORNE

Honor and majesty surround him;
strength and beauty fill his sanctuary.

PSALM 96:6 NLT

An Invitation

Are you tired? Worn out? Burned out on religion? Come to me.
Get away with me and you'll recover your life. I'll show you
how to take a real rest. Walk with me and work with me—
watch how I do it. Learn the unforced rhythms of grace.
I won't lay anything heavy or ill-fitting on you. Keep company with me
and you'll learn to live freely and lightly.

MATTHEW 11:28–30 MSG

[God] is looking for people who will come in simple dependence
upon His grace, and rest in simple faith upon His greatness.
At this very moment, He's looking at you.

JACK HAYFORD

Come, all you who are thirsty,
come to the waters;
and you who have no money,
come, buy and eat!
Come, buy wine and milk
without money and without cost.
Why spend money on what is not bread,
and your labor on what does not satisfy?
Listen, listen to me, and eat what is good,
and your soul will delight in the richest of fare.
Give ear and come to me;
hear me, that your soul may live.

ISAIAH 55:1–3 NIV

*C*ome with me by yourselves to a quiet place and get some rest.

MARK 6:31 NIV

God Is for Us

Don't be afraid, I've redeemed you.
I've called your name. You're mine.
When you're in over your head, I'll be there with you.
When you're in rough waters, you will not go down.
When you're between a rock and a hard place,
it won't be a dead end—
Because I am God, your personal God,
The Holy of Israel, your Savior.
I paid a huge price for you...!
That's how much you mean to me!
That's how much I love you!

ISAIAH 43:1–4 MSG

Our days are filled with tiny golden minutes with eternity in them.
Our lives are immortal. One thousand years from this day
you will be more alive than you are at this moment. There is a future
life with God for those who put their trust in Him.

BILLY GRAHAM

Let him who walks in the dark,
who has no light,
trust in the name of the LORD
and rely on his God.

ISAIAH 50:10 NIV

_If_ God is for us, who can be against us?

ROMANS 8:31 NKJV

Wait for the Promises

We must wait for God, long, meekly, in the wind and wet,
in the thunder and lightning, in the cold and the dark.
Wait, and He will come.

FREDERICK W. FABER

Peace does not dwell in outward things but in the heart
prepared to wait trustfully and quietly on Him who has all things
safely in His hands.... Jesus had perfect trust in His Father,
whose will He had come to accomplish. Nothing touched
Him without His Father's permission. Nothing touches
me without my Father's permission.
Can I not then wait patiently? He will show the way.

ELISABETH ELLIOT

A wise gardener plants his seeds, then has the good sense
not to dig them up every few days to see if a crop is on the way.
Likewise, we must be patient as God brings the answers...
in His own good time.

QUIN SHERRER

The Scriptures give us hope and encouragement
as we wait patiently for God's promises to be fulfilled.

ROMANS 15:4 NLT

The way may at times seem dark, but light will arise,
if you trust in the Lord, and wait patiently for Him.

ELIZABETH T. KING

God makes a promise—faith believes it,
hope anticipates it, patience quietly awaits it.

You Satisfy My Soul

In comparison with this big world, the human heart is only
a small thing. Though the world is so large, it is utterly unable
to satisfy this tiny heart. Our ever growing soul and its capacities
can be satisfied only in the infinite God. As water is restless until
it reaches its level, so the soul has no peace until it rests in God.

SADHU SUNDAR SINGH

Whom have I in heaven but you?
And earth has nothing I desire besides you.
My flesh and my heart may fail,
but God is the strength of my heart
and my portion forever.

PSALM 73:25–26 NIV

God bless you and utterly satisfy your heart...with Himself.

AMY CARMICHAEL

They shall neither hunger nor thirst,
Neither heat nor sun shall strike them;
For He who has mercy on them will lead them,
Even by the springs of water He will guide them.

ISAIAH 49:10 NKJV

We are made for God, and nothing less will really satisfy us.

BRENNAN MANNING

Jesus said, "I am the Bread of Life. The person who aligns with me hungers no more and thirsts no more, ever."

JOHN 6:35 MSG

A Quiet Spirit

Don't ever let yourself get so busy that you miss those little
but important extras in life—the beauty of a day...
the smile of a friend...the serenity of a quiet moment alone.
For it is often life's smallest pleasures and gentlest joys
that make the biggest and most lasting difference.

A quiet place is a good place to find out God's angle on any problem.

JANETTE OKE

Don't be concerned about the outward beauty of fancy hairstyles,
expensive jewelry, or beautiful clothes. You should clothe yourselves
instead with the beauty that comes from within, the unfading beauty
of a gentle and quiet spirit, which is so precious to God.

1 PETER 3:3–4 NLT

Year by year the complexities of this spinning world grow
more bewildering, and so each year we need all the more
to seek peace and comfort in the joyful simplicities.

He who dwells in the secret place of the Most High
Shall abide under the shadow of the Almighty.
I will say of the LORD, "He is my refuge and my fortress;
My God, in Him I will trust."

PSALM 91:1–2 NKJV

The fruit of our placing all things in His hands
is the presence of His abiding peace in our hearts.

HANNAH WHITALL SMITH

Depths of the Spirit

"No eye has seen, no ear has heard, no mind has conceived
what God has prepared for those who love him"—
but God has revealed it to us by his Spirit. The Spirit searches all things,
even the deep things of God. For who among men knows the thoughts
of a man except the man's spirit within him? In the same way no one
knows the thoughts of God except the Spirit of God. We have not
received the spirit of the world but the Spirit who is from God,
that we may understand what God has freely given us.

1 CORINTHIANS 2:9–12 NIV

Praise is a place for God to be. A home place. A workshop
for His Holy Spirit in our lives. It is an atmosphere of total openness
where He can be free to do good things in and through our days.

GLORIA GAITHER

The grace of the Lord Jesus Christ, and the love of God,
and the communion of the Holy Spirit be with you all. Amen.

2 CORINTHIANS 13:14 NKJV

_____

_____

_____

_____

_____

_____

_____

_____

_____

_____

_____

_____

_____

_____

_____

_____

_____

_____

_____

_____

_____

_____

*God knows the rhythm of my spirit
and knows my heart thoughts.
He is as close as breathing.*

Sanctuary of the Soul

Deep within us all there is an amazing inner sanctuary of the soul,
a holy place, a Divine Center, a speaking Voice, to which
we may continuously return. Eternity is at our hearts,
pressing upon our time-torn lives, warming us with intimations
of an astounding destiny, calling us home unto Itself.

THOMAS R. KELLY

The soul is like a wild animal—tough, resilient, resourceful,
savvy, self-sufficient. It knows how to survive in hard places.
But it is also shy. Just like a wild animal, it seeks safety
in the dense underbrush. If we want to see a wild animal,
we know that the last thing we should do is go crashing through the
woods yelling for it to come out. But if we will walk quietly
into the woods, sit patiently by the base of the tree, and fade into
our surroundings, the wild animal we seek might put in an appearance.

PARKER PALMER

As for God, his way is perfect;
the word of the LORD is flawless.
He is a shield for all who take refuge in him.

PSALM 18:30 NIV

*W*ithin each of us there is an inner place where the
living God Himself longs to dwell, our sacred center of belief.

Whispered Prayer

We do not need to search for heaven, over here or over there,
in order to find our eternal Father. In fact, we do not even need to speak
out loud, for though we speak in the smallest whisper
or the most fleeting thought, He is close enough to hear us.

TERESA OF AVILA

We can go through all the activities of our days in joyful awareness
of God's presence with whispered prayers of praise and adoration
flowing continuously from our hearts.

RICHARD J. FOSTER

I need not shout my faith. Thrice eloquent
Are quiet trees and the green listening sod;
Hushed are the stars, whose power is never spent;
The hills are mute: yet how they speak of God!

CHARLES HANSON TOWNE

God doesn't need us to shout.
We can whisper and He still hears our prayers.

GARY SMALLEY AND JOHN TRENT

There is a time for everything, and a season
for every activity under heaven...
a time to be silent and a time to speak.

ECCLESIASTES 3:1, 7 NIV

*E*very whispered prayer sent heavenward
is our response to God's embrace.

JANET L. SMITH

Wisdom of Silence

We are silent at the beginning of the day because God should have the
first word, and we are silent before going to sleep because
the last word also belongs to God.

DIETRICH BONHOEFFER

I want you woven into a tapestry of love, in touch with everything
there is to know of God. Then you will have minds confident
and at rest, focused on Christ, God's great mystery.
All the richest treasures of wisdom and knowledge
are embedded in that mystery and nowhere else.

COLOSSIANS 2:2-3 MSG

Being able to bow in prayer as the day begins or ends gives expression to
the frustrations and concerns that might not otherwise be ventilated. On
the other end of that prayer line is a loving heavenly Father
who has promised to hear and answer our petitions.

DR. JAMES DOBSON

He calms the storm,
So that its waves are still.
Then they are glad because they are quiet;
So He guides them to their desired haven.

PSALM 107:29-30 NKJV

*I*t is a good discipline to wonder in each new situation
if people wouldn't be better served by our silence than by our words.

HENRI J. M. NOUWEN

The Music of God

From the heart of God comes the strongest rhythm—
the rhythm of love. Without His love reverberating in us,
whatever we do will come across like a noisy gong or a clanging symbol.
And so the work of the human heart, it seems to me,
is to listen for that music and pick up on its rhythms.

KEN GIRE

Like art, like music, like so many other disciplines,
prayer can only be appreciated when you actually spend time in it.
Spending time with the Master will elevate your thinking.
The more you pray, the more will be revealed. You will appreciate
not only the greatness of prayer, but the greatness of God.

JONI EARECKSON TADA

Life is what we are alive to. It is not length but breadth....
Be alive to...goodness, kindness, purity, love, history, poetry,
music, flowers, stars, God, and eternal hope.

MALTBIE D. BABCOCK

Let God have you, and let God love you—and don't be surprised
if your heart begins to hear music you've never heard and
your feet learn to dance as never before.

MAX LUCADO

_S_ing songs to the tune of his glory,
set glory to the rhythms of his praise.

Time Well Spent

Being present with someone I love is never a waste of time,
especially if God is the one with whom I am present.
Martha complained about Mary wasting time at Jesus' feet
while work piled up.... Indeed, any time spent in prayer seems wasted
to someone who has priorities other than a relationship with God.
For one who loves God, however, there is no more
productive, or necessary, act.

PHILIP YANCEY

Mary...was sitting at Jesus' feet and listening to him teach.
But Martha was busy with all the work to be done. She went in
and said, "Lord, don't you care that my sister has left me alone
to do all the work? Tell her to help me." But the Lord answered her,
"Martha, Martha, you are worried and upset about many things.
Only one thing is important. Mary has chosen the better thing,
and it will never be taken away from her."

LUKE 10:39–42 NCV

Life in the presence of God should be known to us
in conscious experience. It is a life to be enjoyed
every moment of every day.

A. W. TOZER

God is never in a hurry but spends years
with those He expects to greatly use.

L. B. COWMAN

Blessings Await

We walk without fear, full of hope and courage and strength
to do His will, waiting for the endless good which He is always giving
as fast as He can get us able to take it in.

GEORGE MACDONALD

God is waiting for us to come to Him with our needs....
God's throne room is always open.... Every single believer
in the whole world could walk into the throne room all at one time,
and it would not even be crowded.

CHARLES STANLEY

The LORD longs to be gracious to you;
he rises to show you compassion.
For the LORD is a God of justice.
Blessed are all who wait for him!

ISAIAH 30:18 NIV

You are never alone. In your heart of hearts, in the place
where no two people are ever alike, Christ is waiting for you.
And what you never dared hope for springs to life.

ROGER OF TAIZÉ

*L*ift up your eyes. Your heavenly Father waits to bless you—
in inconceivable ways to make your life
what you never dreamed it could be.

ANNE ORTLUND

Learning to Listen

Part of our job is simply to be...always attentive to what we are doing and
what is going on inside us, at the same time we listen
and pay attention to the people and events around us. Part of our job
is to expect that, if we are attentive and willing, God will
"give us prayer," will give us the things we need,
"our daily bread," to heal and grow in love.

ROBERTA BONDI

Doing something for you,
bringing something to you—
that's not what you're after.
Being religious, acting pious—
that's not what you're asking for.
You've opened my ears so I can listen.

PSALM 40:6 MSG

If we knew how to listen, we would hear Him speaking to us.
For God does speak.... If we knew how to listen to God, if we knew
how to look around us, our whole life would become prayer.

MICHAEL QUOIST

Jesus is always waiting for us in silence. In that silence,
He will listen to us, there He will speak to our soul,
and there we will hear His voice.

MOTHER TERESA

The more faithfully you listen to the voice within you,
the better you will hear what is sounding outside.

DAG HAMMARSKJÖLD

Nature's Silent Beauty

Experience God in the breathless wonder and startling beauty
that is all around you. His sun shines warm upon your face.
His wind whispers in the treetops. Like the first rays of morning light,
celebrate the start of each day with God.

WENDY MOORE

God is here! I hear His voice
While thrushes make the woods rejoice.
I touch His robe each time I place
My hand against a pansy's face.
I breathe His breath if I but pass
Verbenas trailing through the grass.
God is here! From every tree
His leafy fingers beckon me.

MADELEINE AARON

Silently one by one, in the
infinite meadow of heaven
blossomed the lovely stars,
the forget-me-nots of the angels.

HENRY WADSWORTH LONGFELLOW

O Lord, what a variety of things you have made!
In wisdom you have made them all. The earth is full of your creatures.

PSALM 104:24 NLT

For Himself

Although it is good to think upon the kindness of God,
and to love Him and worship Him for it,
it is far better to gaze upon the pure essence of Him
and to love Him and worship Him for Himself.

Stand up and praise the LORD your God.... You alone are the LORD.
You made the heavens, even the highest heavens,
and all their starry host, the earth and all that is on it,
the seas and all that is in them. You give life to everything,
and the multitudes of heaven worship you.

NEHEMIAH 9:5–6 NIV

We desire many things, and God offers us only one thing.
He can offer us only one thing—Himself.
He has nothing else to give. There is nothing else to give.

PETER KREEFT

The reason for loving God is God Himself,
and the measure in which we should love Him
is to love Him without measure.

BERNARD OF CLAIRVAUX

*J*oy is perfect acquiesce in God's will because
the soul delights itself in God Himself.

H. W. WEBB-PEPLOE

Seek His Face

The person who asks for and seeks this one thing from the Lord
makes his petition confidently and serenely. This is the one,
true and only life of happiness that...we should contemplate
the Lord's graciousness forever.

AUGUSTINE

I have been away and come back again many times to this place.
Each time I approach, I regret ever having left. There is a peace here,
a serenity, even before I enter. Just the idea of returning becomes
a balm for the wounds I've collected elsewhere. Before I can finish
even one knock, the door opens wide and I am in His presence.

BARBARA FARMER

As we practice the presence of God, more and more we find ourselves
going through the stresses and strains of daily activity with an ease
and serenity that amazes even us...especially us.

RICHARD J. FOSTER

The serene beauty of a holy life
is the most powerful influence in the world
next to the power of God.

BLAISE PASCAL

*G*ive thanks to the LORD, call on his name;
Look to the LORD and his strength; seek his face always.

PSALM 105:1, 4 NIV

His Quiet Care

Try to find a quiet place. Outward silence develops
inward silence; and outward silence improves inward silence
as it begins to take root in your life.

MADAME GUYON

Be still, and in the quiet moments, listen to the voice
of your heavenly Father. His words can renew your spirit...
no one knows you and your needs like He does.

JANET L. SMITH

I'm asking GOD for one thing, only one thing:
To live with him in his house my whole life long.
I'll contemplate his beauty;
I'll study at his feet.
That's the only quiet, secure place in a noisy world,
The perfect getaway.

PSALM 27:4-5 MSG

Ask God to help you truly know Him as the Great I AM.
Ask Him to help you lay aside your *to-do* list while you spend
quality quiet time getting to know Him. This way, you can
learn to *be* with Him in everything you *do*.

AMY AND JUDGE REINHOLD

The miracle comes quietly into the mind
that stops an instant and is still.

R. FISHEL

God's Eternal Love

The LORD is like a father to his children,
tender and compassionate to those who fear him.
For he knows how weak we are;
he remembers we are only dust.
Our days on earth are like grass;
like wildflowers, we bloom and die.
The wind blows, and we are gone—
as though we had never been here.
But the love of the LORD remains forever....
The LORD has made the heavens his throne;
from there he rules over everything.

PSALM 103:13–17, 19 NLT

The reason we can dare to risk loving others is that
"God has for Christ's sake loved us." Think of it! We are loved eternally,
totally, individually, unreservedly! Nothing can take God's love away.

GLORIA GAITHER

Great is his love toward us,
and the faithfulness of the LORD endures forever.

PSALM 117:2 NIV

I am wholly His; I am peculiarly His;
I am universally His; I am eternally His.

THOMAS BENTON BROOKS

*Amid the ebb and flow of the passing world,
our God remains unmoved, and His throne endures forever.*

ROBERT COLEMAN

Silent Reverence

A spiritual discipline...is the concentrated effort to create some
inner and outer space in our lives, where...obedience can be practiced.
Through a spiritual discipline we prevent the world from
filling our lives to such an extent that there is no place left to listen.
A spiritual discipline sets us free to pray or, to say it better,
allows the Spirit of God to pray in us.

HENRI J. M. NOUWEN

There are times when to speak is to violate the moment...
when silence represents the highest respect. The word for such times
is reverence. The prayer for such times is "Hallowed be thy name."

MAX LUCADO

Over the margins of life comes a whisper, a faint call,
a premonition of richer living which we know we are passing by.
Strained by the very mad pace of our daily outer burdens,
we are further strained by an inward uneasiness,
because we have hints that there is a way of life vastly richer
and deeper than all this hurried existence,
a life of unhurried serenity and peace and power.

THOMAS R. KELLY

The LORD is in his holy temple;
let all the earth be silent before him.

HABAKKUK 2:20 NIV

Windows of Our Soul

Open wide the windows of our spirits and fill us full of light;
open wide the door of our hearts that we may receive and entertain Thee
with all the powers of our adoration.

CHRISTINA ROSSETTI

Live for today but hold your hands open to tomorrow.
Anticipate the future and its changes with joy. There is a seed
of God's love in every event, every circumstance, every...
situation in which you may find yourself.

BARBARA JOHNSON

Let my soul be at rest again, for the Lord has been good to me....
And so I walk in the LORD's presence as I live here on earth!

PSALM 116:7, 9 NLT

Day-to-day living becomes a window through which we get a glimpse
of life eternal. The eternal illuminates and gives focus to the daily.

JANICE RIGGLE HUIE

To know ourselves loved
Is to have the
Depths of our own
Capacity to love
Opened up.

J. MAIN

*J*ust as there comes a warm sunbeam into every cottage window,
so comes a love—born of God's care for every separate need.

NATHANIEL HAWTHORNE

Alone with God

There is no true, deep conversion, no true, deep holiness,
no clothing with the Holy Spirit and with power, no abiding peace
or joy, without being daily alone with God. What an inestimable
privilege is the institution of daily secret prayer to begin every morning.
Let it be one thing that our hearts are set on.

ANDREW MURRAY

It is not objective proof of God's existence that we want but the
experience of God's presence. That is the miracle we are really after, and
that is also, I think, the miracle that we really get.

FREDERICK BUECHNER

God loves to look at us, and loves it when we will look back at Him. Even
when we try to run away from our troubles...God will find us,
bless us, even when we feel most alone, unsure.... God will find a way
to let us know that He is with us *in this place*, wherever we are.

KATHLEEN NORRIS

The Spirit of prayer makes us so intimate with God that we scarcely pass
through an experience before we speak to Him about it.

OLE HALLESBY

He alone is my rock and my salvation....
Pour out your hearts to him, for God is our refuge.

PSALM 62:6, 8 NLT

The Spiritual Life

The spiritual life is first of all a life. It is not merely something
to be known and studied, it is to be lived.... We live as spiritual people
when we live as people seeking God.
If we are to become spiritual, we must remain human.

THOMAS MERTON

I stayed awake all night,
prayerfully pondering your promise....
You're the closest of all to me, GOD,
and all your judgments true.

PSALM 119:148, 151 MSG

Prayer is the way the life of God is nourished. Our ordinary views
of prayer are not found in the New Testament. We look upon prayer
as a means of getting things for ourselves; the Bible's idea of prayer
is that we may get to know God Himself.

OSWALD CHAMBERS

Prayer is by nature a dialogue between man and God.
It unites the soul with its Creator and reconciles the two.
Its effect is to hold the world together.

JOHN OF THE LADDER

The highest pinnacle of the spiritual life is not joy in unbroken sunshine, but absolute and undoubting trust in the love of God.

A. W. THOROLD

Guided by His Hand

To You, O Lord, I lift up my soul.
O my God, in You I trust....
Make me know Your ways, O Lord;
teach me Your paths.
Lead me in Your truth and teach me,
for You are the God of my salvation;
for You I wait all the day.
Remember, O Lord, Your compassion
and Your lovingkindnesses,
for they have been from of old.

PSALM 25:1–2, 4–6 NASB

We are of such value to God that He came to live among us...
and to guide us home. He will go to any length to seek us,
even to being lifted high upon the cross to draw us back to Himself.
We can only respond by loving God for His love.

CATHERINE OF SIENNA

God guides us.... He leads us step by step, from event to event.
Only afterwards...do we experience the feeling of having been led
without knowing it, the feeling that God has mysteriously guided us.

PAUL TOURNIER

You guide me with your counsel,
leading me to a glorious destiny.

PSALM 73:24 NLT

The Lord is able to guide. The promises cover
every imaginable situation.... Take the hand He stretches out.

ELISABETH ELLIOT

Expressions of Nature

Sunshine spills through autumn-colored leaves, lighting up
their brilliance like stained-glass windows in a great cathedral,
expressing the wonder of God's love, declaring His glory.

If you have never heard the mountains singing, or seen the trees of the
field clapping their hands, do not think because of that they don't.
Ask God to open your ears so you may hear it, and your eyes
so you may see it, because, though few people ever know it,
they do, my friend, they do.

McCandlish Phillips

I see in the stars, in the rivers, I see in the open fields, patches of heaven
and threads of paradise. Let me sew the earth, the day, the way
of my life into a pattern that forms a quilt, God's quilt,
to keep me warm today and always.

Christopher de Vinck

The sunshine dancing on the water, the lulling sound of waves
rolling into the shore, the glittering stars against the night sky—
all God's light, His warmth, His majesty—our Father of light
reaching out to us, drawing each of us closer to Himself.

Wendy Moore

_____

_____

_____

_____

_____

_____

_____

_____

_____

_____

_____

_____

_____

_____

_____

_____

_____

_____

_____

_____

_____

_____

_____

*You will go out in joy and be led forth in peace;
the mountains and hills will burst into song before you,
and all the trees of the field will clap their hands.*

ISAIAH 55:12 NIV

Listening Prayer

Lord, teach me to listen. The times are noisy and my ears are weary with
the thousand raucous sounds which continuously assault them...
let me hear You speaking in my heart. Let me get used to the sound
of Your voice, that its tones may be familiar when the sounds
of the earth die away and the only sound will be the music
of Your speaking voice. Amen.

A. W. TOZER

If we do not listen we do not come to the truth. If we do not pray
we do not even get as far as listening....
Four things go together: silence, listening, prayer, truth.

HUBERT VAN ZELLER

Prayer is not asking. Prayer is putting oneself in the hands of God,
at His disposition, and listening to His voice
in the depths of our hearts.

MOTHER TERESA

God is not interested in you praying perfectly;
He just wants to spend time with you and be able
to speak with you and know you are listening.

DR. HENRY CLOUD

I listen carefully to what God the LORD is saying,
for he speaks peace to his faithful people.

PSALM 85:8 NLT

Stillness of Creation

In the forest we can learn life's lessons if we will—
How to turn towards the sunshine, standing straight and still,
How to be content with slow development and grow
In grace and strength in spite of storms, of wind and frost and snow.

PATIENCE STRONG

In the beginning God created the heavens and the earth....
Then God saw everything that He had made,
and indeed it was very good.... On the seventh day God ended His work
which He had done, and He rested.... Then God blessed the seventh day
and sanctified it, because in it He rested from all His work.

GENESIS 1:1, 31; 2:2–3 NKJV

Nothing in all creation is so like God as stillness.

MEISTER ECKHART

Living becomes an awesome business when you realize
that you spend every moment of your life in the sight
and company of an omniscient, omnipresent Creator.

J. I. PACKER

The day is done, the sun has set,
Yet light still tints the sky;
My heart stands still
In reverence,
For God is passing by.

RUTH ALLA WAGER

*N*ature has been for me, for as long as I can remember, a source of solace, inspiration, adventure, and delight.

LORRAINE ANDERSON

Lover of My Soul

Solitude is a place inside myself where God's Spirit and my spirit dwell together in union. This place within me is private and reserved for the intimacies that God and I share. What happens between the two of us in that place is not meant for public consumption. It is a place where I can give myself with abandon to the Lover of my soul.

RUTH HALEY BARTON

If you are seeking after God, you may be sure of this:
God is seeking you much more. He is the Lover,
and you are His beloved. He has promised Himself to you.

JOHN OF THE CROSS

Time passed in silence with God is time spent growing
in relationship with Him. And time spent letting His love
flow through you to others is an investment in eternity.

AMY AND JUDGE REINHOLD

You are in the Beloved...therefore infinitely
dear to the Father, unspeakably precious to Him.
You are never, not for one second, alone.

NORMAN DOWTY

The LORD is righteous in all his ways and loving toward all he has made.
The LORD is near to all who call on him, to all who call on him in truth.

PSALM 145:17–18 NIV

His Dwelling Place

In Solomon's day God dwelt in a temple made of stone;
today He dwells in a temple composed of living believers.
When we really see that God has made our hearts His dwelling place,
what a deep reverence will come over our lives!

WATCHMAN NEE

Imagine yourself as a living house. God comes in to rebuild that house....
You thought you were going to be made into a decent little cottage:
but He is building a palace. He intends to come and live in it Himself.

C. S. LEWIS

You are living stones that God is building into his spiritual temple.
What's more, you are his holy priests.

1 PETER 2:5 NLT

The soul is a temple, and God is silently building it by night and by day.
Precious thoughts are building it; unselfish love is building it;
all-penetrating faith is building it.

HENRY WARD BEECHER

We cannot kindle when we will
The fire that in the heart resides
The spirit bloweth and is still
In mystery our soul abides.

MATTHEW ARNOLD

_If_ each moment is sacred—
a time and place where we encounter God—
life itself is sacred.

JEAN M. BLOMQUIST

Taste and See

If we begin to worship and come to God again and again
by meditating, by reading, by prayer, and by obedience, little by little God
becomes known to us through experience. We enter into a sweet familiar-
ity with God, and by tasting how sweet the Lord is
we pass into...loving God, not for our own sake, but for Himself.

BERNARD OF CLAIRVAUX

All [God's] glory and beauty come from within, and there He
delights to dwell. His visits there are frequent, His conversation sweet, His
comforts refreshing, His peace passing all understanding.

THOMAS À KEMPIS

I come to the garden alone
while the dew is still on the roses,
And the voice I hear, falling on my ear,
the Son of God discloses.

He speaks, and the sound of His voice
is so sweet the birds hush their singing.
And the melody that He gave to me
within my heart is ringing.

And He walks with me, and He talks with me,
and He tells me I am his own.
And the joy we share as we tarry there
none other has ever known.

C. AUSTIN MILES

*O*pen your mouth and taste, open your eyes and see—how good God is.
Blessed are you who run to him.

PSALM 34:8 MSG

In Silent Strength

A living, loving God can and does make His presence felt,
can and does speak to us in the silence of our hearts, can and does warm
and caress us till we no longer doubt that He is near, that He is here.

BRENNAN MANNING

The sound of "gentle stillness" after all the thunder and wind have passed
will be the ultimate Word from God.

JIM ELLIOT

The wonder of living is held within the beauty of silence, the glory
of sunlight...the sweetness of fresh spring air, the quiet strength of earth,
and the love that lies at the very root of all things.

God walks with us.... He scoops us up in His arms or simply sits
with us in silent strength until we cannot avoid
the awesome recognition that yes, even now, He is here.

GLORIA GAITHER

Open my eyes that I may see
Glimpses of truth Thou hast for me.
Place in my hands the wonderful key
That shall unclasp and set me free:
Silently now I wait for Thee,
Ready, my God, Thy will to see;
Open my eyes, illumine me, Spirit divine!

CLARA H. SCOTT

You're my place of quiet retreat; I wait for your Word to renew me.

Rest in the Lord

Rest is not idleness, and to lie sometimes on the grass under the trees on a summer's day, listening to the murmur of water, or watching the clouds float across the sky, is by no means a waste of time.

SIR JOHN LUBBOCK

God provides resting places as well as working places. Rest, then, and be thankful when He brings you, wearied, to a wayside well.

L. B. COWMAN

True silence is the rest of the mind; it is to the spirit what sleep is to the body: nourishment and refreshment.

WILLIAM PENN

Relax, everything's going to be all right;
rest, everything's coming together;
open your hearts, love is on the way!

JUDE 1:2 MSG

Joy comes from knowing God loves me and knows who I am and where I'm going...that my future is secure as I rest in Him.

DR. JAMES DOBSON

A life of inward rest and outward victory
is the inalienable birthright of every child of God.

HANNAH WHITALL SMITH

Peace Be Still

Peace is not placidity: peace is
The power to endure the megatron of pain
With joy, the silent thunder of release,
The ordering of Love. Peace is the atom's start,
The primal image: God within the heart.

MADELEINE L'ENGLE

Peace I leave with you, My peace I give to you; not as the world gives
do I give to you. Let not your heart be troubled, neither let it be afraid.

JOHN 14:27 NKJV

Calm me O Lord as you stilled the storm,
Still me O Lord, keep me from harm.
Let all the tumult within me cease,
Enfold me, Lord, in Your peace.

CELTIC TRADITIONAL

Unceasing Prayer has a way of speaking peace to the chaos.
Our fractured and fragmented activities begin focusing
around a new Center of Reference. We experience peace,
stillness, serenity, firmness of life orientation.

RICHARD J. FOSTER

The time, how lonely and how still
Peace shines and smiles on all below
The plain, the stream, the wood, the hill
All fair with evening's setting glow.

AMISH HYMN

Christ is the still point of the turning world.

T. S. ELIOT

Open Your Heart

The "air" which our souls need also envelops all of us at all times
and on all sides. God is round about us in Christ on every hand,
with many-sided and all-sufficient grace.
All we need to do is to open our hearts.

OLE HALLESBY

Jesus Christ opens wide the doors
of the treasure house of God's promises, and bids us go in
and take with boldness the riches that are ours.

CORRIE TEN BOOM

Life begins each morning.... Each morning is the open door
to a new world—new vistas, new aims, new tryings.

LEIGH MITCHELL HODGES

The steadfast love of the Lord never ceases, his mercies never come
to an end; they are new every morning; great is your faithfulness.

LAMENTATIONS 3:22–23 NRSV

I can drink freely of God's power and experience His
touch of refreshment and blessing—much like
an invigorating early spring rain.

ANABEL GILLHAM

*Faith goes up the stairs that love has made
and looks out the window which hope has opened.*

CHARLES H. SPURGEON

Sacred Moments

We are always in the presence of God.... There is never
a non-sacred moment! His presence never diminishes.
Our awareness of His presence may falter, but the reality
of His presence never changes.

MAX LUCADO

I lie awake thinking of you,
meditating on you through the night.
Because you are my helper,
I sing for joy in the shadow of your wings.
I cling to you; your strong right hand holds me securely.

PSALM 63:6−8 NLT

The ability to see and the practice of seeing God and God's world comes
through a process of seeking and growing in intimacy with Him.

DALLAS WILLARD

Live in me. Make your home in me just as I do in you. In the same way
that a branch can't bear grapes by itself but only by being joined
to the vine, you can't bear fruit unless you are joined with me.

JOHN 15:4 MSG

Simplicity will enable you to leap lightly. Increasingly you will
find yourself living in a state of grace, finding...the sacred
in the ordinary, the mystical in the mundane.

DAVID YOUNT

The reflective life is a way of living that heightens
our spiritual senses to all that is sacred.

KEN GIRE

Inward Prayer

Walk and talk and work and laugh with your friends.
But behind the scenes, keep up the life of simple prayer
and inward worship. Let inward prayer be your last act
before you fall asleep and the first act when you awake.

THOMAS R. KELLY

Those who live prayerfully are constantly ready to receive
the breath of God, and to let their lives be renewed and expanded.

HENRI J. M. NOUWEN

Prayer is like love. Words pour at first. Then we are more silent
and can communicate in monosyllables. In difficulties
a gesture is enough, a word, or nothing at all—love is enough.
Thus the time comes when words are superfluous....
The soul converses with God with a single loving glance.

CARLO CARRETTO

Enter into the inner chamber of your mind. Shut out all things
save God and whatever may aid you in seeking God;
and having barred the door of your chamber, seek Him.

ANSELM OF CANTERBURY

I ponder all your great works
and think about what you have done.
I lift my hands to you in prayer.
I thirst for you as parched land thirsts for rain.

PSALM 143:5–6 NLT

All good meditative prayer
is a conversion of our entire self to God.

THOMAS MERTON

Our Soul and Spirit

The very life of God, epitomized in the love of God,
originates only and always with Him.... It does not...
spring from the soil of our own souls and spirits.

W. PHILIP KELLER

God's holy beauty comes near you, like a spiritual scent,
and it stirs your drowsing soul.... He creates in you the desire
to find Him and run after Him——to follow wherever He leads you,
and to press peacefully against His heart wherever He is.

JOHN OF THE CROSS

In the very beginning it was God who formed man by His Word.
He made man in His own image. God was spirit and He gave man
a spirit so that He could come into Him and mingle
His own life with man's life.

MADAME JEANNE GUYON

The soul is a breath of living spirit, that with excellent sensitivity,
permeates the entire body to give it life. Just so, the breath
of the air makes the earth fruitful. Thus the air
is the soul of the earth, moistening it, greening it.

HILDEGARDE OF BINGEN

*W*ho you are and what you've done are all we'll ever want.
Through the night my soul longs for you.
Deep from within me my spirit reaches out to you.

ISAIAH 26:8–9 MSG

You Are There

I look behind me and you're there,
then up ahead and you're there, too—
your reassuring presence, coming and going.
This is too much, too wonderful—
I can't take it all in!

PSALM 139:5–6 MSG

I believe that God is in me as the sun is in the color and fragrance
of a flower—the Light in my darkness, the Voice in my silence.

HELEN KELLER

Where can I go from your Spirit?
Where can I flee from your presence?
If I go up to the heavens, you are there;
if I make my bed in the depths, you are there.
If I rise on the wings of the dawn,
if I settle on the far side of the sea,
even there your hand will guide me,
your right hand will hold me fast.

PSALM 139:7–10 NIV

Know by the light of faith that God is present,
and be content with directing all your actions toward Him.

BROTHER LAWRENCE

I am with you and will watch over you wherever you go.

GENESIS 28:15 NIV

Faithful Promises

Great faith isn't the ability to believe long and far into the misty future.
It's simply taking God at His word and taking the next step.

JONI EARECKSON TADA

Now faith is being sure of what we hope for and certain
of what we do not see.... By faith we understand that the universe
was formed at God's command, so that what is seen was not made out
of what was visible.... And without faith it is impossible to please God,
because anyone who comes to him must believe that he exists
and that he rewards those who earnestly seek him.

HEBREWS 11:1, 3, 6 NIV

God takes care of His own. He knows our needs.
He anticipates our crises. He is moved by our weaknesses.
He stands ready to come to our rescue. And at just the right moment He
steps in and proves Himself as our faithful heavenly Father.

CHARLES SWINDOLL

*L*et us draw near to God.... Let us hold unswervingly
to the hope we profess, for he who promised is faithful.

HEBREWS 10:22–23 NIV

His Inward Voice

Retire from the world each day to some private spot.... Stay in the secret
place till the surrounding noises begin to fade out of your heart
and a sense of God's presence envelops you.... Listen for the inward Voice
till you learn to recognize it.... Give yourself to God and then be what and
who you are without regard to what others think....
Learn to pray inwardly every moment.

A.W. TOZER

Prayer is
The world in tune,
A spirit-voice,
And vocal joys
Whose *echo* is heaven's bliss.

HENRY VAUGHN

God is not really "out there" at all. That restless heart, questioning who
you are and why you were created, that quiet voice that keeps calling
your name is not just out there, but dwells in you.

DAVID AND BARBARA SORENSEN

Come, let us worship and bow down.
Let us kneel before the LORD our maker,
for he is our God.
We are the people he watches over,
the flock under his care.
If only you would listen to his voice today!

PSALM 95:6–7 NLT

Joy is the echo of God's life within us.

JOSEPH MARMION

Reflections of God

Just as a prism of glass miters light and casts a colored braid,
a garden sings sweet incantations the human heart strains to hear.
Hiding in every flower, in every leaf, in every twig and bough,
are reflections of the God who once walked with us in Eden.

The heavens proclaim the glory of God.
The skies display his craftsmanship.
Day after day they continue to speak;
night after night they make him known.
They speak without a sound or word;
their voice is never heard.
Yet their message has gone throughout the earth,
and their words to all the world.

PSALM 19:1–4 NLT

Woven in a perfect way, a blanket of stars covers the night sky,
each star set in its place, reflecting its perfect light. All the stars together
make a grand display, glimmering and shimmering
in a unique expression of praise to the Creator of them all.

WENDY MOORE

I see nature…playing endless variations in design and beauty….
In such simple yet eloquent ways, I am reminded that God is personal,
revealing Himself continuously in the finite.

JUDITH LECHMAN

The tiniest dewdrop hanging from a grass blade in the morning
is big enough to reflect the sunshine and the blue of the sky.

Guideposts

To be glad of life, because it gives you the chance to love
and to work and to play and to look up at the stars; to be satisfied
with your possessions, but not contented with yourself until you have
made the best of them;...to think seldom of your enemies,
often of your friends, and every day of Christ; and to spend
as much time as you can, with body and with spirit
in God's out-of-doors—these are little guideposts
on the footpath to peace.

HENRY VAN DYKE

We do not understand the intricate pattern of the stars in their courses,
but we know that He who created them does, and that just as surely as He
guides them, He is charting a safe course for us.

BILLY GRAHAM

A new path lies before us;
We're not sure where it leads;
But God goes on before us,
Providing all our needs.
This path, so new, so different
Exciting as we climb,
Will guide us in His perfect will
Until the end of time.

LINDA MAURICE

The signposts of GOD are clear and point out the right road.
The life-maps of GOD are right, showing the way to joy.

PSALM 19:7–8 MSG

Friendship with God

O the pure delight of a single hour
that before Thy throne I spend,
When I kneel in prayer, and with Thee, my God,
I commune as friend with friend!

FANNY J. CROSBY

Friendship with God is a two-way street.... Jesus said that He tells
His friends all that His Father has told Him; close friends communicate
thoroughly and make a transfer of heart and thought. How awesome
is our opportunity to be friends with God, the almighty Creator of all!

BEVERLY LAHAYE

God-friendship is for God-worshipers;
They are the ones he confides in.

PSALM 25:14 MSG

Meditation is the activity of calling to mind, and thinking over,
and dwelling on, and applying to oneself, the various things that one
knows about the works and ways and purposes and promises of God.
It is an activity of holy thought, consciously performed
in the presence of God, under the eye of God, by the help of God,
as a means of communion with God.

J. I. PACKER

_God's friendship is the unexpected joy we find
when we reach for His outstretched hand._

JANET L. SMITH

New Life of Love

So, chosen by God for this new life of love, dress in the wardrobe God
picked out for you: compassion, kindness, humility, quiet strength,
discipline. Be even-tempered, content with second place,
quick to forgive an offense. Forgive as quickly and completely
as the Master forgave you. And regardless of what else you put on,
wear love. It's your basic, all-purpose garment. Never be without it.

COLOSSIANS 3:12–14 MSG

Look deep within yourself and recognize what brings life
and grace into your heart. It is this that can be shared
with those around you. You are loved by God.
This is an inspiration to love.

CHRISTOPHER DE VINCK

When God's power touches a mere human being, something happens!
Creation all over again! The life-changing touch of love!

GLORIA GAITHER

Faith in God gives your life a center from which you can
reach out and dare to love the world.

BARBARA FARMER

*L*ove others for the sake of God.
Love God for His own sake.

AUGUSTINE

Gift of the Ordinary

We encounter God in the ordinariness of life, not in the search
for spiritual highs and extraordinary, mystical experiences,
but in our simple presence in life.

BRENNAN MANNING

May our lives be illumined
by the steady radiance
renewed daily,
of a wonder,
the source of which
is beyond reason.

DAG HAMMARSKJÖLD

Why is everyone hungry for more?...
I have God's more-than-enough,
More joy in one ordinary day
Than they get in all their shopping sprees.
At day's end I'm ready for sound sleep,
For you, God, have put my life back together.

PSALM 4:6–8 MSG

The sun...in its full glory, either at rising or setting—
this, and many other like blessings we enjoy daily;
and for the most of them, because they are so common,
most men forget to pay their praises. But let not us.

IZAAK WALTON

The incredible gift of the ordinary!
Glory comes streaming from the table of daily life.

MACRINA WIEDERKEHR

Walking with God

My Lord God, I have no idea where I am going.
I do not see the road ahead of me. I cannot know for certain
where it will end.... But I believe that the desire to please You
does in fact please You. And I hope I have that desire
in all that I am doing. I hope that I will never do anything apart
from that desire. And I know that if I do this, You will lead me
by the right road though I may know nothing about it.

Therefore will I trust You always, though I may seem to be lost
and in the shadow of death. I will not fear, for You are ever with me.
And You will never leave me to face my perils alone.

THOMAS MERTON

God gets down on His knees among us; gets on our level
and shares Himself with us. He does not reside afar off
and send diplomatic messages, He kneels among us....
God shares Himself generously and graciously.

EUGENE PETERSON

Yet I am always with you;
you hold me by my right hand.

PSALM 73:23 NIV

Breath of the Soul

As prayer moves into the subconscious mind, breathed longings
of wonder and adoration seem always underneath
and in the background of everything—a little like a tune that we
suddenly realize we have been humming all day long.

RICHARD J. FOSTER

God says to His children: Are you lonesome? Breathe out My name.
Come to Me and I will be your friend. Are you sick? Come to Me
for healing. Are you left out of things? Feeling rejected
and pushed aside? Come home to Me.

ALICE CHAPIN

So faith bounds forward to its goal in God,
and love can trust her Lord to lead her there;
upheld by Him my soul is following hard,
till God hath full fulfilled my deepest prayer.

FREDERICK BROOK

I love the LORD because he hears my voice
and my prayer for mercy.
Because he bends down to listen,
I will pray as long as I have breath!

PSALM 116:1–2 NLT

*P*rayer is the breath of the soul.

OLE HALLESBY

Contemplating God

We are so preciously loved by God that we cannot
even comprehend it. No created being can ever know how much
and how sweetly and tenderly God loves them. It is only with the help
of His grace that we are able to persevere in spiritual contemplation with
endless wonder at His high, surpassing, immeasurable love
which our Lord in His goodness has for us.

JULIAN OF NORWICH

Take a moment to consider the awesome reality that the God
who spoke and created the universe is now speaking to you. If Jesus could
speak and raise the dead, calm a storm...and heal the incurable, then what
effect might a word from Him have upon your life?

HENRY T. BLACKABY

When I look at the night sky and see the work of your fingers—
the moon and the stars you set in place—
what are mere mortals that you should think about them,
human beings that you should care for them?

PSALM 8:3–4 NLT

*C*ontemplation is nothing else but a secret, peaceful,
and loving infusion of God, which, if admitted,
will set the soul on fire with the spirit of love.

JOHN OF THE CROSS

Nature's Retreat

The deep woods reveal God's presence. The way the golden sunlight
streaks through the lush greens and browns of a summer wood
is nothing short of divine. In the fall the profusion of colors
makes every leaf a prayer. Winter's snow transforms the woods
into a cathedral. Even the dark, drab hues of the woods
in early spring speak of hope and resurrection. It is a place
where I can be on a spiritual retreat.

RAYMOND K. PETRUCCI

I love to think of nature as an unlimited broadcasting station through
which God speaks to us every hour, if only we will tune in.

GEORGE WASHINGTON CARVER

If we are children of God, we have a tremendous treasure in nature
and will realize that it is holy and sacred. We will see God reaching out to
us in every wind that blows, every sunrise and sunset, every cloud
in the sky, every flower that blooms, and every leaf that fades.

OSWALD CHAMBERS

For great is your love, reaching to the heavens;
your faithfulness reaches to the skies.
Be exalted, O God, above the heavens;
let your glory be over all the earth.

PSALM 57:10–11 NIV

The more I study nature,
the more I am amazed at the Creator.

LOUIS PASTEUR

Step by Step

Our Heavenly Father...wants us to reach up and take His hand,
but He doesn't want us to *ever* let go. In fact, His desire is that we
become *more* and *more* dependent upon Him for every step.
That's because He wants to take us to places we've never been.
To heights we can't even imagine.... God always requires the first step
to be ours. In order to take that first step, we must look into
the face of God, reach up and take His hand,
and say, "Lead me in the path You have for me, Lord.
From this day on I want to walk with You."

STORMIE OMARTIAN

Whoso draws nigh to God
One step through doubtings dim,
God will advance a mile
In blazing light to him.

Your walk with God is essential. His heart is not seen
in an occasional chat or weekly visit. We learn His will
as we take up residence in His house every single day.

MAX LUCADO

For we walk by faith, not by sight.

2 CORINTHIANS 5:7 NKJV

The Lord's goodness surrounds us at every moment. I walk through it almost with difficulty, as through thick grass and flowers.

R. W. BARBER

God's Living Word

For the word of God is living and active and sharper
than any two-edged sword, and piercing as far as the division of soul
and spirit, of both joints and marrow, and able to judge the thoughts
and intentions of the heart. And there is no creature hidden
from His sight, but all things are open and laid bare to the eyes
of Him with whom we have to do.

HEBREWS 4:12–13 NASB

With my whole heart have I sought You;
Oh, let me not wander from Your commandments!
Your word I have hidden in my heart,
that I might not sin against You.

PSALM 119:10–11 NKJV

Every part of Scripture is God-breathed and useful
one way or another—showing us truth, exposing our rebellion,
correcting our mistakes, training us to live God's way.
Through the Word we are put together
and shaped up for the tasks God has for us.

2 TIMOTHY 3:16–17 MSG

When we give the Word of God space to live in our heart, the Spirit of God will use it to take root, penetrating the earthiest recesses of our lives.

KEN GIRE

Joy in His Presence

We must drink deeply from the very Source the deep calm
and peace of interior quietude and refreshment of God,
allowing the pure water of divine grace to flow plentifully
and unceasingly from the Source itself.

MOTHER TERESA

When God finds a soul that rests in Him and is not easily moved,
He operates within it in His own manner. That soul allows God to do
great things within it. He gives to such a soul the key to the treasures He
has prepared for it so that it might enjoy them. And to this same soul He
gives the joy of His presence which entirely absorbs such a soul.

CATHERINE OF GENOA

What extraordinary delight we find in the presence of God.
He draws us in, His welcome so fresh and inviting.

As we keep his commands, we live deeply and surely in him,
and he lives in us. And this is how we experience his deep
and abiding presence in us: by the Spirit he gave us.

1 JOHN 3:24 MSG

A quiet morning with a loving God puts the events
of the upcoming day into proper perspective.

JANETTE OKE

Ellie Claire® Gift & Paper Expressions
Brentwood, TN 37027
EllieClaire.com
Ellie Claire is a registered trademark of Worthy Media, Inc.

Be Still and Know that I Am God
Promise Journal
© 2014 by Ellie Claire
Published by Ellie Claire, an imprint of Worthy Publishing Group, a division of
Worthy Media, Inc.

ISBN 978-1-63326-009-2

Scripture references are from the following sources: The Holy Bible,
New International Version®, NIV®. Copyright © 1973, 1978, 1984 by Biblica, Inc.™
Used by permission of Zondervan. All rights reserved worldwide. The New King James
Version (NKJV). Copyright © 1982 by Thomas Nelson, Inc. Used by permission. The New
American Standard Bible® (NASB). Copyright © 1960, 1962, 1963, 1968, 1971, 1972, 1973,
1975, 1977, 1995 by The Lockman Foundation. Used by permission. The New Revised
Standard Version Bible (NRSV). Copyright 1989, 1995, Division of Christian Education of
the National Council of the Churches of Christ in the United States of America. Used
by permission. The Holy Bible, New Living Translation (NLT), copyright 1996, 2004.
Used by permission of Tyndale House Publishers, Inc., Wheaton, Illinois. *The Message*
(MSG). Copyright © 1993, 1994, 1995, 1996, 2000, 2001, 2002 by Eugene Peterson. Used
by permission of NavPress, Colorado Springs, CO. The New Century Version® (NCV).
Copyright © 1987, 1988, 1991 by Thomas Nelson, Inc. Used by permission. All rights
reserved.

Excluding Scripture verses and deity pronouns, in some quotations references
to men and masculine pronouns have been replaced with gender-neutral
or feminine references.

Compiled by Barbara Farmer
Cover and interior design by Gearbox | studiogearbox.com

Printed in China.

3 4 5 6 7 8 9 – 19 18 17 16 15